## Also by Toni Thomas:

*Chosen*
*Fast as Lightening*
*Walking on Water*
*Blue Halo*
*Ace Raider of the Unfathomable Universe*
*You'll be Fast as Lightning Coveting my Painted Tail*
*Hotsy Totsy Ballroom*
*Love Adrift in the City of Stars*
*In the Pink Arms of the City*
*In the Kingdom of Longing*
*The Things We Don't Know*
*In the Boarding House for Unclaimed Girls*
*They Became Wing Perfect and Flew*
*Unburdened Kisses*
*Bandits Come and Remove Her Body in the Night*
*There is This*
*Here*
*The Smooth White Vanishing*
*Perishing in the Rain*
*A Different Measure of Moonlight*
*The Secret Language of River*
*Inside Her a River of Snow was Traveling*
*The Arbiter of Her Own Flame*
*Paradise on a Shoestring*
*A Bride of Amazement*
*A Portuguese Lullaby is What I am After*
*In the Hermitage of the Soul*

# You can Cast Around Forever in my Father's Shoes

Published 2025
Annalese Press
West Yorkshire HD9 3XZ
England

Copyright © 2025 Toni Thomas

All rights reserved. No part of this publication may be reproduced, stored, or transmitted in any form, or by any means electronic, mechanical or photocopying, recording or otherwise, without the express written permission of the publisher.

Design, layout and illustrations by
Peter Wadsworth
*Young man seated with hands folded on knees*
*Amedeo Modigliani*, 1918

*British Library Cataloguing-in-Publication Data*
A catalogue record for this book is available on request from the British Library.

ISBN 978-1-0685744-6-7

# Contents

## Part One - *Weaving*

| | |
|---|---|
| My father is dragging his left leg | 3 |
| He wants to forget | 5 |
| You have written the history of your life | 6 |
| Gift | 8 |
| The Barrel of Death | 10 |
| Convinced | 12 |
| Fragile | 13 |
| Ball Practice | 15 |
| You are buttoning up | 16 |
| Shrimp | 18 |
| Your sentences | 20 |
| Very soon | 21 |
| Back then | 23 |
| Today the rings of Saturn | 24 |
| You are a destiny with death | 26 |

## Part Two - *A Bruised Sunset*

| | |
|---|---|
| You can cast around forever | 31 |
| The stop dashes | 33 |
| If my tooth | 34 |
| I have been searching out | 35 |
| My father gave his vow to protect | 37 |
| Sometimes my left leg | 38 |

| | |
|---|---:|
| When my father married my mother | 39 |
| Every spring | 40 |
| When he waves goodbye | 41 |

## Part Three - *Secret Wish List*

| | |
|---|---:|
| He wants to keep the gerbil | 45 |
| When you question him | 46 |
| You wear a spotted jacket | 47 |
| This boy kneels | 48 |
| His father's hands smell of gasoline | 49 |
| You like to wander the shops | 50 |
| You are wearing the astronaut costume | 51 |
| The nuns offer up lessons | 52 |
| You refuse to swallow | 53 |
| You are rinsing out words | 54 |
| In the forest | 55 |
| If you had gone to school | 56 |

## Part Four - *In the Story*

| | |
|---|---:|
| The good soldier | 61 |
| Heat scours the pavement | 62 |
| You have known a lifetime | 63 |
| You conquer the girl | 64 |
| When the vanquished birds | 65 |
| His hands are immaculate | 66 |
| You hold your voice | 67 |

| | |
|---|---|
| I am translating you | 68 |
| You kiss the spotty sky | 69 |
| It is never shrew bread | 70 |
| And what can you tell me | 71 |
| In the storied universe | 72 |
| No one rakes the field | 73 |

## Part Five - *Saying Goodbye*

| | |
|---|---|
| When my father dies | 77 |
| You might think | 78 |
| A man on a mission | 79 |
| You can ice my father's forehead | 80 |
| If luck has been fingering | 81 |
| You claim | 83 |
| We have grown attached | 84 |
| Last night | 85 |
| Some things speak soft | 86 |
| Please plant a seed | 87 |
| Once the house unbinds | 88 |
| You are sighing | 89 |
| You are saying goodbye | 90 |
| You are calling back | 91 |
| You have always been | 92 |
| My father carries a cross | 93 |
| I won't always need to coax | 94 |
| In my sleep | 95 |
| In the clear light of the early dawn | 96 |
| In the dry mouth of the day's cottonwoods | 99 |

| | |
|---|---|
| I want you to last forever | 100 |
| My father collected coins and stamps | 101 |
| Were you always the knobby groom | 103 |
| You cast your eye over the field | 104 |
| Were there times | 105 |

## Part Six - *The Welcoming Forest*

| | |
|---|---|
| My father is holding a candle | 109 |
| My father would gift give | 110 |
| What does the word *naught* stand for | 111 |
| Things come and go | 112 |
| When mercy comes | 115 |
| Your polestar is waiting | 116 |
| A diamond cutter's apprentice | 117 |
| My father has always said *when my boat comes in* | 118 |
| More than the wounded soldier | 121 |
| In real life | 122 |
| No more blurred kiss | 123 |
| Farewell | 124 |
| Farewell my Soldier | 125 |
| I can move on now | 126 |
| Listen | 127 |
| Can innocence set up | 128 |
| Can days always be this calm | 129 |
| Back then | 130 |
| Are there shorelines | 131 |
| My father is combing the dark | 132 |
| Glory | 133 |

*What did I know, what did I know
of love's austere and lonely offices*
                                        Robert Hayden

            *the silence
            then the rain
         dashing its silver seeds
           against the house*
                            Mary Oliver

# Part One

*Weaving*

## My father is dragging his left leg

that is all flame
no one calls him the blind mule
blue zephyr
notices the slumped chord in his eyes
way he sometimes stab things
then serves up an éclair

no one offers him a bread box
factory foreman job
so he can live with his more resonate
not feel left out

no one says *childhood is dangerous*
abuse maims
it is hard to grow old in America
be a thin cup married to pills.

He has never learned to ride a bike
joke at the table
was sexually abused by
his drunken father's girlfriend
moved twelve times in high school.

He is dragging his left foot
the one that no longer minds

will rattle the dark mercurial
curse my onion field till it bleeds.

For nearly a century
he has slept his body on this earth.
A remarkable feat.
How many times did he fold
childhood into a paper plane
search god in the sky
the soft measure
of a mother?

## He wants to forget

the way money talks
politicians preen
power turns prize
a person with a high IQ
but spotty schooling
can seem incidental
nameless

leans on sharp written editorials
the tenets of the constitution
card playing, Highland Games
girls dancing a jig in tartan.

The dependable bill payer
Army vet, jazz lover
my father scrupulously shaves his face
slips into a laundered shirt, slacks
changes another catheter

lets folks keep their view
of the world as a playground
place where no one drowns
is left homeless
unseen.

You have written the history of your life

inside Ella, bird feeders
will not trouble the neighbors for a ride
if your legs ache
ask to join their Friday night joy party
will not measure the footsteps it takes
to hobble across the highway, bag groceries
drag them from store to home
will not insist folks come and visit
listen to Coltrane
sample your mango chutney.

You have written the history of your life
inside newspapers, penned editorials
that work to name the sly and the decent
will not stick your nose uninvited
into neighbors' business
have learned how to act small, self sufficient
cram a boy's loveliness into the camera box
with the scratched lens
can generate your own play station
cork the tidal wave of your room
till it barely leaks.

You have written the history of your life
inside postcards, carefully pressed coins
stamps, jazz albums
inside donations to wounded soldiers, tribes
children's hospitals, pandas, bird sanctuaries, trees

written your history inside limited edition plates
where pink rouged children get to run
toss ball, dodge kisses

still remember your grandchildren's birthdays
launder your sheets, towels, slacks
bake pie, keep track of the Yankees
the Peace Summit going on in Europe
still continue to write the history of your life
in hushed vowels
have managed to outlive two wives, an only son
stay the brave aviator
tall man in a crisp shirt.

At 90 years old you still know
when the blood red moon is coming
your favorite streets in Manhattan
lines from the poem *Annabel Lee*
still remember the hike up Mount Washington
with your new love
before that my mother's slinky body
remember last year's World Series
your favorite recipe for shepherd's pie

still open your face into a loose grin
swoon over summer's first scent of magnolia
your blueberry bushes flush with fruit.

## Gift

You loosen the dirt
unbind weed
plant rows of tomatoes
plump beefeaters, romas for the sauce
cherry sized for the salad
plant them in full sun
come August will pick diligently.

They are for my mother
the woman you secretly worship
the tomato lover
to be diced into her omelet
lathed with mayo on the toast
propped with mixed greens, arugula.

All summer you complain
about the heat, your lost job, children
the plague of bugs, greed
things you'd never do for yourself
but do for this woman you've married
the ex-lifeguard, once painter
who used to wear slinky gowns
now works retail
has shored up pin money for a patio pool
the prospect of water

this woman who slides into her swimsuit
every evening, weekend

twirls in the lime green tube
as if she is sixteen
invites you, against your will
to stop what you're doing
jump in.

## The Barrel of Death

You speak well to the strawberries
hand water your peonies
bait the yellow finch to perch nearby
don't want to load the barrel of death
with your bullets

over the years have become
accustomed to being solitary
the guy with the steady handshake
never sick postal employee
used to what the world takes
won't always give back

now don't worry so much
if the doctor over prescribes pills
the bananas aren't ripe
the trailer park bakes in the noonday sun
car horns blare at you loud as applause.

You don't want to load
the barrel of death with your bullets
speak decent to the prostate cancer
your catheters, lack of sleep
claim even if the country is going to hell
you still have your Yankees, haggis, German strudel
the noontime sun creeping in through your window

still have corned beef, spicy mustard, good coffee
one more pinochle game to look forward to
maybe a next.

You don't want to load
the barrel of death with your bullets
at ninety years old bury them
inside a crop of memories
the worship of your dead son

offer up coffee cake
to your one and only daughter
then crush her heart
with the sum of her failed life.

Convinced

your pedigree is Scottish
you search the Thomas clan
want to be buried
to the sound of bagpipes

tell me you once had tweed cloth
cut to order, made into a suit
on that tourist trip up to Aberdeen.

At 88 years old will take two buses
walk the steep half mile uphill
to the Scottish Highland Games
come July
if nobody is around
willing to take you.

# Fragile

You are weaving the course of your days
in small steps, jobs, disposable catheters
talk the faults in the electoral college
the Soup Friday started up in the park
talk Pictionary, wonder how it gets played
say you're getting anxious
have a lot to think about
like missing the step, losing your change
your online account passwords
doctor appointments, meds
tell me the weather is forecast for heavy rain
snow in Edinburgh
ask about the freeze.

At 88 years old nothing comes easy
you say you fell yesterday on the way home
after depositing your election ballot
fell again in the neighbor's ornamental pond
couldn't get up so crawled your way to a car
were worried about getting back from the market
when the service desk wouldn't cash your check
you forgot your bus ticket was good for two hours.

Many people have promised to look in on you
but their days get busy.
You will work hard not to trouble them

ask for favors
have spent a lifetime learning not to expect
wish for phone calls that never come.

You spend hours with newspapers
tending the cat, listening to jazz
have an active mind in an old person's body
don't want to spend Thanksgiving alone
while I'm in Edinburgh
hope secretly someone will take pity
invite you in.

Ball Practice

You have been doing it
all your life
slamming balls left field, right field
out of the stadium
sometimes crack the bat
when your fist turns willful
have spent years running bases
keeping a scorecard in your pocket

ignore my brother's loyalty to the Red Sox
his stack of ball cards
the way at Little League games
he spits in the dirt like a pro
stares down the pitcher
hoping you will notice.

You have been doing ball practice
all your life
hate excuses, injuries
players that exit the field, don't come back
hold a penchant for underdogs
that left fielder who comes out of nowhere
becomes the league's big upset
sudden inheritor of an ace batting average
trophies.

## You are buttoning up

the same dress shirt as yesterday
but I'm not saying
don't want you to feel judged
the forgetful child in a strict room.

It is April in the Northwest
the sun a tease
that turns spiteful.
You have your prize plants to nurse
a cat that's not eating

have tethered yourself to card games
things that occupy the mind
keep hands busy
middle of the night roast chicken, potatoes
check baseball comments on Twitter
while most folks sleep.

It is not easy to be 90 and fading away.
Not easy to know your cat may not outlive you
the seniors in the trailer park double bolt their doors
seem resigned to narrow lives
friendships tight as a noose.

Tomorrow you will bring sponge cake, pudding
over to the clubhouse for the noon game
like doing this, feeling useful.

Bring the food as an offering
later shake your head
tell me most of it comes back untouched
as if nobody's hungry.

## Shrimp

You are shelling a bucket of them
their bodies the coral pink
of a girl's first dance dress
want nothing to go missing
peel them slow under the cold faucet
will sauté with onion, garlic, pepper

are making this dish for my children
the fussy eaters you rarely see
want them to catch a whiff of your table's joy field
have bought pepsi, sprite, club soda just in case.

You are from the Bronx, an old man
with not a lot of time left or money.
It is extravagant that you have
so many shrimp in the bucket
of your trailer park kitchen
their hard shells being peeled one by one
to marry the sauce and the pasta

have bought them from the guy
who parks his truck down by the gas station
sells iced cod, crab, shrimp, sometimes salmon.
The guy with an upper front tooth missing
who can't afford the repair.
*He's a good man* you say
talks baseball, the kid he's putting through
community college, talks chorizo pizza

the best place to get it
how the landscape is burnt brown
thanks to the drought.

You are peeling shrimp
unlike the way you have slowly over time
peeled my voice bare
no, you are peeling them delicate
the way we prize young girls in waiting
petals not destined for the trash.

Your sentences

veer between aerial flight
and a ruined city
between high minded patriot
and weary soldier
can squeeze words into combat
paragraphs into artillery.

You have taken yourself to many places
yet still feel left out
the forgotten boy
but won't tell anybody this
the pain that lurks inside your dress shirt
behind the firm resolve of your lips

no, just shuffle across the highway
haul your bags of groceries
fry the potato, meat, onions
check your two rose bushes
to see if their hearts still beat.

## Very soon

my father may not remember
which shoe goes on which foot
where the canned soup gets kept
why his blue dress shirt is missing

may not remember the way to the bathroom
the season batting average of the Yankees
which way his key turns
the name for a winged creature
great bids of pinochle
his favorite variety of Tillamook ice cream

very soon my father may no longer be able
to watch late night news, read the newspaper
hobble from kitchen to couch
fry sausage, bacon
switch on his laptop, find emails
may no longer be able to install catheters
take them out.

My father has done his best
to survive a brutal childhood
not vanish
married a saucy woman
bought a house, raised two kids
worked three jobs and night college
buried his wife, only son, married a second
nursed her through ALS

when she could no longer walk, talk, eat
has been the good bill payer, tax citizen
three times Army enlistee
ex-postal worker, coupon clipper.

He shaves his face, tidies up, puts on a clean shirt
will not burden you with his troubles
wants to believe the world still holds
frilled poppies, small farms, decency
no one gets forgotten
labeled *useless*.

Back then

she says you laughed a lot
weren't afraid to look foolish
stand on one foot
bought her a stuffed monkey
clutch of roses

says you were handsome till your hair fled
loved corned beef, pistachio ice cream
hole in the wall restaurants, handball
your Yankees, Broadway matinees, the Rockettes
could turn the dark into a Coney Island
wonder wheel.

She says at first it was easy
the army chalet in Bavaria, maid service
days bicycling through villages
hikes up snowcapped peaks.

Later, stateside, the tiny flat
in a three family house
two young children
your night college, six day a week jobs.
Still later the impatience
the burnt potato casseroles, black inked walls
bowl after bowl
of fudge marble ice cream.

Today the rings of Saturn

will spin speechless in a blind place
you will cross the highway slow
with your bags of milk, sausage, bagels
cross while the cars steam anxious

today you will fry bacon
drizzle the fat over your potato salad
quietly look back on the hard years
turn them into meatloaf
Nat King Cole
marshmallow jello for the noon game.

At intervals you will slide
your catheters in and out
down antibiotics to fight another infection
ride to the city doctor
check on your cancerous prostrate

you will say nothing
about the sexual abuse
endless schools, alcoholic dad, orphanage
glass case of army metals
years overseas, the second world war
just stir the creamer into your coffee

will say nothing about my mother
how at first, before her young death

she clung to the roses of you
tried to gather you up
call you home
to a different measure of beauty.

You are a destiny with death

but nobody is saying.
I try to organize help
a cleaner, grocery delivery
but you are particular
certain days, certain ways
and no imposing
have outrun your past
but will not be able to
outrun the future.

You can recite the Founding Fathers' pledge
Bill of Rights
pulse public decency from your pen
have buried two wives, my brother
made it this far
after a life of hard work

and despite how much my heart
has known shattered glass on a mute string
my hat goes off to you for coming this far
89 years old - intact, near indomitable
your mind agile
playing pinochle with seniors
four sessions a week
hour after hour alone evenings, mealtimes
your catheters, cancerous prostate

infection after infection
the falls, bruises, aches and pain
the way you carry on, adjust
no desire to pull the plug, exit early
before the toughest part sets in.

# Part Two

*A Bruised Sunset*

## You can cast around forever

in my father's hard shoes
they hold flame
under a brown lid
eat algae, bugs
the world's boggy
have kept him almost incorruptible
while the dark heaves.

*Don't make me go in* I beg
as he drags my body into the pond
insists I learn amphibian
how to sink or swim by my own juices.
I am afraid I will drown
inside his chaste eye
that gobbles debris
unctuous children.

My father is the color of want
what gets spent
what gets left for dead.
Nobody listens
places more than a perfunctory ear
to his voice.

You can cast around forever
in my father's hard shoes

become stillborn
pregnant in contaminated water
never impose prison
onto the fate
that's been ascribed to you.

The stop dashes

in the middle of my sentence
make no sense to my father
nor my poems with a heavy dose
of the dark sloshing.

The daydreams in my bed
made no sense to my father
nor the stuffed rabbit, doll clothes
crayons scattered across the carpet
nor the girl sewing lacy trim
onto her tattered slip.

The perilous in my voice
the one dipped in the river
uncertain of answers
makes no sense to my father
nor the girl who looks into the big forest
and feels small.

The wounds in my father
the too many jobs, dismissals
subway platforms
anonymous
are like coins that rattle
inside his pocket
without a name.

If my tooth

needs to be yanked out of its socket
my father's hand will be the steady blade
his theory –
better to go toothless then rattle on
about the ache.

If I use a word that is half curved
a spill of summer's pink ice
no use setting my heart to its sheen
while his dictionary wags
an instruction manual.

If I bow to his dark pudding
stroke the smooth
crew-cut my mouth
will the trapped birds in my heart
break free
fly away
unbroken?

I have been searching out

jars of good pickles for my father
most of my life
not the bland artificial kind
the over sugared, dipped in dye
but kosher ones he will truly savor.

He's always claimed there's nothing quite
like the crunch of a good dill
the kind swimming with peppercorns
a tad sweet, but mostly a lean of sour.
I want him to be pleased
not remind me of my near disasters
my pie eyed and poems.

My father is on the last rung of his life
won't complain about the prostate cancer
neighbors at his trailer park who never stop by
won't talk about death – that nasty word
while the iris are blooming
a Chinese dance troupe is here to perform
that good saxophonist arrives on Thursday.

Just as in childhood when I reached down
deep into the oak barrel of our Queens deli
attempting to fish him out the perfect treat
I have been seeking good pickles

for my father most of my life.
Sometimes he says my taste buds are useless.
Sometimes I make a home run with the pickles
find him a jar he claims *aren't half bad.*

# My father gave his vow to protect

gave his hurts, creased hands
curved back
worked hard to lift mountains
stir the sea into a backwater.

My father kept us in school shoes
sheltered with roof, pork chops
braised liver, ice cream
set up a ping pong table
in the broken down garage

showed us how to walk
mile after mile
without our feet aching
hold the world at distance
forage the past till it
spills out razors.

My father could mollify want
snap a brick in two
lobotomize sunset
turn our yard beetles
into a fetish of flame.

## Sometimes my left leg

refuses to listen
while the right waits clairvoyant
knows exactly where I need to go.
It can feel like some slumped fantasy
tethered to a tightrope.
How many words end in road kill
how many failed marriages
are an emblem of the body's dissonance?

September can be a time to
peel back  memories
that scratch inside without a future
a time to dry petals between pages
slow down words
blaze crisp as the autumn leaves
less fearful.

I once thought relationships
stay loyal
don't have to beg for a meal
thought no one needs clairvoyance
to mind the future
the one of a kind stand for something
more than a perfect egg
sewed shut eulogy.

I once thought I would always be here
willing to listen.

# When my father married my mother

she'd already run off west with a stuntman
had her first marriage annulled by German relations.
He was the Marlon Brando double in an army uniform
about to be sent off to Bavaria.
My mother, the fiery once lifeguard
who loved horses, paints, ball gowns
sewn to a lonely boy early shoved in an orphanage
later forced to have sex with his father's girlfriend.
Who would have thought it would last.

There are stories that are hard to tell
for a very long time stay locked in a suitcase
but won't lay flat.
When my father married my mother
he had nothing to give but his losses, his kisses
his thin dreams, ticket to Bavaria.

There are unlikely matches in this world
hopeful ones that turn into detritus.
Wounds that go underground and bleed.
You could say I am the product
of half risen trellises
pummeled kisses
a bruised sunset.

## Every spring

my father dug in manure
pruned back the bushes
hatched praying mantis, ladybugs
to prosper the yard.

Every spring my father
clipped clutches of lilac
placed them in a slim vase
for my bedside table.

I'd come home tired, hungry
open my door to the indecent
scent of lilac

so that now, every May
on my evening walk with the dog
I search out lilac
snatch branches that drape
over the churchyard fence
carry them home
as psalm.

## When he waves goodbye

I fear for my father's safety
the precarious that sometimes
passes for decent

when he kisses me on the cheek
then scolds
I fear for his lip's blurred flame

when he welcomes me back
I am afraid of the ice fields
bracken
the way his face can cut like a blade.

And as for mealtime
when he sets the table
drowns me in the apology of a pot roast
don't think I can take my fork
and eat from it
without those sledgehammers
of the dark
still ringing.

# Part Three

*Secret Wish List*

## He wants to keep the gerbil

it is the only pet he has ever known
but then storage lockers don't listen.

He is nearly nine
has come back from the orphanage
to a strange apartment.
The father says *get used to it*
unfolds the boy's bedroll.
Outside the snow is falling.
It is December, nearly Christmas.

The boy knows better than to ask
for more than his share
knows things go missing
his father has made a friend
of bar stools, women
that late night he must
guide him home.

The boy will not pray for luck
just look after his one coat
a day's worth of warmth
made of sweat and blood
an exiled Jesus.

When you question him

about sums on the blackboard, history
have him confess to the extra potato
stolen at table
make the day seem like a fantasy of
seamless love in a pitted landscape

when you scrub out his mouth
place those treacle words on his tongue
don't think he'll dance as a monkey forever
forgive your hand's strict rehearsal
the slaps you sometimes waged
in the name of calm

don't think you have taught things right
the tamed pony in a circus
no, recognize for once
the shy, the lonely in him
how this boy will go on to walk through
the pages of his life angry
and barely seen.

You wear a spotted jacket

grey shoes
wear your heart indoors.

When the dark comes
the streets turn malice
when the sails of your voice
go missing
who will come to you
light a candle

keep your father's girlfriend away
who will rise up from
their bar stool
bigger than a fruit bat
rescue?

This boy kneels

with a pocket of pale wishes
below the stained glass of Mary.

He has come here
empty handed
dreams a good watch
decent shoes
eyeglasses

wants the world to listen
to his periled body

not as chained bread
in the breadbox
but soft.

## His father's hands smell of gasoline

under the nails, sawdust and glue.
He has sold off the boy's pet gerbil.
Locked his wishes inside another suitcase
another move to a voiceless apartment.

When night comes there will be
only barstools
the boy reaching out his hand
to lead his father back
to the cold comfort of their beds.

But the boy has youth
riding in his pocket
hopes bigger than destiny
will take the stones
on his tongue

turn them into a job
sardine sandwich, sneakers
military uniform
words inked and stretched
out of a blue casket.

## You like to wander the shops

see into windows as if the world
nests a carved carousel
pastel painted prophecy

run around the city
delivering theatre tickets
so you can buy yourself glasses
see without the blur.

You know enterprise
a holiday tree missing
nuns forgetful of patience
know what it feels like to
mess up shoe laces
get your ears boxed.

Who could have known you'd
move through so many years
ninety of them
still hold a secret wish list
still be looking for love
a place to call *home*.

## You are wearing the astronaut costume

from the Salvation Army store.
It is Halloween when children
count on tricks, candy in the bag
instead of razors.
You will do what the nuns say
clip your voice in the name of Jesus
not muddy your one pair of shoes.

You are wearing the astronaut outfit
the tired one that boasts tin foil, a helmet
is meant for a rusted spaceship.

Will anyone notice beneath the foil
this blood on your hands
this boyhood tethered to loss
so thick you have no idea
how to name it?

## The nuns offer up lessons

how to set table, eat right with fork
damp down the voice
keep your one pair of shoes
from mucky.

You have been here before
slept with truculent angels
tried to worship your father
the German widower who
prefers bar stools over his son.

The day knows how to please
itself on small rations
do a handstand for a knob of cheese.

No wonton past will deter
a boy with spit in his polish
a worker bee state of mind.

You have entered the forest
with your wobbly flashlight
refuse to admit what it's like
to feel lost.

You refuse to swallow

the pills given
are labeled the brazen boy
in a sea of compliance
and every act you usher in
will be seen as a middle finger
that refuses to lay flat.

When childhood is a
series of knife blades
does the blue hurt of a boy's eyes
get sucked dry by the river
does it turn him into a rescuer
of forgotten things
tribes, animals, causes?

In your voice
are broken toys
a lonely apartment
your father staggering
the nun's harsh tutelage
your one pair of decent shoes
beaten down.

You are rinsing out words

the ones born of a nail bed
rinsing out your underwear.

It is nearly Sunday
when the clutch of hard pews
hold you
your voice gets pinched into
a chorus of pert angels.

You have been taught how to launder
eat meals without fuss
take the heel end of the bread
and bless it.

But someday when the birds fly in
and your father returns
will there be only the forest
the well of your past washed clean

the sudden rustle of your mother
calling you home?

In the forest

animals wander
paw prints litter the path
holding the pine scented
resin of his mother.

The boy has stolen bread
from the nun's kitchen.
He is just seven
too young to know the way
some fates carry a cage.

April is a sky without teardrops.
The chores the boy has escaped
do not come after him
and as for his father
the man who keeps losing keys
jobs, bottles, the boy
there will always be
this welcoming of the trees
this camouflage of leaves
the boy hides in.

## If you had gone to school

in the other neighborhood
the one with pressed shirts, blue blazers
the good lunch ticket
not needed to move so much
if you had a parent looking after you

would your life have turned out different
would the song of your heart
be sung in another key
would my mother, my brother
have not died of the so many defeats
they couldn't bear?

If you had gone to school
in the other neighborhood
would you have learned to speak smooth
not brood or deride things
learned about the stars, galaxies
Faulkner, Steinbeck
taken your gift for writing
and found new friends?

If you had gone to school
in the other neighborhood
belonged to something
were seen by your teachers
as not just the kid who turns up
midterm then moves

if the nuns hadn't squashed Jesus
into a glass vial and orphanages
were a foreign planet

if you had known some permanence
if your mother hadn't died
your father was not a collector of bottles
your only sibling had not been sent out west
would your life be a different story

would my brother and I have traveled
the ample of you
not the less
turned out with lives
that didn't carry a sorrow so deep
we barely knew how to contain it?

# Part Four

*In the Story*

## The good soldier

in the story
becomes a product
of contamination
walks the earth
destined to search
for his lost mother.

In the story
no shoe will ever fit right
the daughter holds a broken key
sunset is spiteful.

In the story
there is no shelter
you take and take
don't measure the cost
she buries her heart
in a death camp
speechless.

Heat scours the pavement

manhandles the paint
infernos the child's wagon
till it's too hot to pull.

In the story
there are escarpments
pardons, parasites
the one armed, infirm

the sun pasted onto
a fringed landscape
fondled by lupine

in the story
the house gets peeled raw
inside the strict of your voice
everything turns into
a stammer of hurricanes.

You have known a lifetime

of being the motherless groom
ready to squelch what is foreign
render a girl with stab wounds.

So tell me
what stopgaps the voice
from climbing its hymn notes

who will rub the daughter
bright as a polished stone
wash her in God's love
till your harsh eye
turns empty

wash the past into a pool
of moonlit women
the innocent river?

## You conquer the girl

till she grows
sallow then timid
laps cake batter
turns a charm bracelet
into your curse

but not all stories
become tar pitch
sometimes a girl spits out
the Shrove Thursday on her tongue
learns to listen

set up her own deathbed
not as mortuary
but vacant lot
repository
for tired bones
shy roses.

When the vanquished birds

come back untroubled
come back as more than fantasy
more than starvation
the burdensome death
come back flush with forgiveness

will the phlox remember
the shy of your soul
in the sway of the sweet grass

will every evening
begin and end
soft?

His hands are immaculate

never need to scour the field
bury beetles in a sea of kerosene.

Every grove hums with hazelnuts
when the rain comes
he drinks from it
leaves the girl a forest of dreams.

In the story the man's hands
are immaculate
he would never suck her voice
her body dry
pilfer.

## You hold your voice

a well of dark water
consecrating the night.

I am afraid to speak
tear open this veil
that conceals me

live in the corn husks
the poplar
ink stained hands.

If I retch this veil
will your anguish leave
will the day
the cosmos
rise up
fold my lament
into meadow?

I am translating you

into a new tongue
beyond name calling
translating you into bird call
a canopy of trees
stars grazing.

You are old now
sit at the table curved
can't reach the ground easy
to tie shoes
remember the name
of that first orphanage

but still prick the skin
of the tapioca pudding
with your spoon
proclaim it *a feast*.

You kiss the spotty sky

and birds fly
the field unbuckles
a blue horizon
crystal rosary.

In the story
you are leavened bread
intricate hieroglyphs
when the wolf comes
you are ready
toss fear
into the brambles.

Every sunset flirts
beyond the named
supplants famine
with flame.

It is never shrew bread

placed on the girl's tongue
only the sky's fauna.

In the story
she can speak with temerity
and still the earth listens
words unbind
the haltered past turns
a scalloped edge.

See how the future
flutters and foams
the calm of the dark feels
all the women in silky hose
red dresses
permissioned to come back.

And what can you tell me

about early morning
the white forest
bark peeled away from the birch
the way sunlight befriends
a handwritten note can hold
the clemency of roses

what can you tell me about
ironed kisses and the ones
that hide in a basement

what can you tell me about
decency
the child torn from a parent's arms
hope sired from sludge

what can you tell me
about unbound places
the voice as a turnstile
how the snow in winter
still marries a tired landscape
in the name of love?

In the storied universe

that is soothe and surprise
not all sums are countable
people compress, sink, float
genuflect beyond the desolate.

In the storied universe
the old man on the bench
finds a voice
fireflies flirt
train tickets arrive out of nowhere
the Polish couple in the park
keep dancing.

In the storied universe
that is not this one
there is room
there is always room
even a marooned boy
can dig his original voice
out of the bog.

No one rakes the field

paupers the day
to keep the night hostage
lovers come back
not on a mission to blind
but filial as a house
with pearled sheets.

In the story
the girl carries a fistful of plums
learns to walk soft
follow her own traces
the night splashes her hem with violet

and as for the women
they call to her
call to her
from the river
in a voice that is all singing.

# Part Five

*Saying Goodbye*

When my father dies

will the body of the night
open wide to receive him
his neighbors pay respect
press their hands
into a pose of birds mating
uncork a bottle
drink to his life

will the world stand still
pause in its frantic rectory
reminisce about his shy ways
passion for food, exploration, decency
how his body managed to hobble
across streets, up and down stairs
tend the garden
even in his last days

will we remember his clumsy jokes
thin jacket, news clippings
gift trays of pudding, tacos, strudel
the way he picked up the dinner tab
grateful for anybody willing to visit

will we remember?

You might think

my father is a withered man
almost invisible
in the field of cars

miss his tenacity, worth
as he paddles from store to store
jokes with the doctors

stays up late night
then slides into another day

savors his cereal, coffee
leans his body toward death
with no complaints.

A man on a mission

my father mows the grass
feeds the birds their measure of suet
pinches off the spent
head of roses.

His voice is yet to learn
how to choir a cathedral
make the past into a braid
of sweet grass.

If you see him on a Monday
or Wednesday or weekend
don't think his youth has fled
that what he utters is nonsense

take in the breath of his life's
sweet buns and litter
take in the way the sky still
works to befriend him
how he has managed to outlive
so many hard things
stay glued.

## You can ice my father's forehead

till the pain stops
the memory of his dead wives
lost son
lonely mealtimes

set him up in a house with shade
where someone finally teaches him
how to ride a bike
smooth the anger that haunts
like a crusty blade

can comb his hair soft
show him a world of lace and folk tales
where rabbits sip tea
the dark lodges snowflakes
out in the cold a couple kiss

you can smooth my father's brow
listen to his recordings of Ella
sample his lamb stew
pumpkin cheesecake

give him a bit of time
as if the journey's not just for the nimble
nobody's meant to be left out
this moment counts.

## If luck has been fingering

my father's life
it is a fickle friend prone to mishaps
the mother who dies of pneumonia
father sheltered by bar stools
orphanage nun who knows how to smack
only son dropped dead in a motel room
the first wife whose heart splinters
the second one stricken with ALS
till he will feed her, wheel her, dress her
help her remember the sway of the trees
scent of the ocean.

If luck has been fingering my father's life
it turns out to be nuanced, an unruly angel
his back recovers from the surgery
so he can walk miles to buy groceries, pay bills
the prostate cancer steadies its pace
the lump on his lung doesn't shout too loud
his birdbath refills out the front door
two blueberry plants bear enough fruit for cereal
the strawberry vines offer up a dessert dish

even now, ninety years old
the gods of mercy continue to visit
the Northwest rain ushers in lilac
orioles return to the feeder
his stove sizzles with ham and eggs, chili

pudding from the torn thumbs of the bread loaf
the day persists to stay local
another hand of pinochle
his newspaper
ballgames.

## You claim

you've never had a bad dream
get visited by your deceased wives
or find my dead brother waiting.
Sometimes all of you gather in the field
set up a foil barbecue, transistor radio
munch sausage, potato salad, cake.
My mother tries to get you to samba
your second wife rattles on about Long Island.

You say the weather there is always decent
no one snowballs the house
stuffs love into a straightjacket

and as for your mother
she goes unmentioned
is the secret wish in your back pocket
the one you have never known
who'll someday carry you home.

## We have grown attached

to each other, me to your stubborn
you to my want to please, then willful
the way you rehearse death
spit it out
insist on the Czech movie Friday night
that one and only Chinese restaurant
on corned beef hash fried crisp without the egg
German potato salad, no mayo.

You type editorials, collect stamps
recognize there are no guarantees
things happen
ask we be more than a blind ball player
complacent.

We have grown used to each other
you the old man of my blood
father figure I only half know
man who derides me
then sprinkles care packages.

Tell me then – what will the world become
without you
who will beseech me
call my name out of the thick dark
kiss me on the cheek then lecture
who will call my name
as if life is more than a gamble?

Last night

you dreamt your second wife
my mom and brother
were at the beach with you.
You tossed ball
chowed down ham sandwiches, chips.
The weather was agreeable
the sun's magnet sucking
the weight of your bodies.

I like to imagine this.
Your good dream.
How sleep can be a comforting refuge
slow forage
one dipped finger at a time
into the unknown valley
of death.

## Some things speak soft

don't penal colony what they send
some velocities take the trees
the pinned sheets
the turkey shed
strangle.

But can stab wounds hold
more than just mortuary
hold a life beyond the pale?

So then give me back the moon
the stars
that child buried in the timothy
give me back her voice
the one gone missing
and missionary blood
the dowager's diligence

give back the future
beyond stampedes
every season washed clean
alive
trustworthy.

Please plant a seed

in my heart
that will not flee
place where my father's body
no longer aches mercury
but meadow.

Please plant a seed
so he can come right
unclip his voice
listen to the shy
the unnamed
prophecy of fountains.

Even when I ate
that soiled cake
chucked it down the toilet
some part of me
was elsewhere

recognized it as
the rub of famine.

## Once the house unbinds

the cages empty
my plate returns to the promise of bread
will you tell me about more than
the climate of potency
toys that spin on a dime, never shatter
tell me about more than treatise
the capable hand, perfect orchid

talk about the secret life of cake
bandy man burdened with cancer
how loss feels, the thick of it
when it condemns the dark to a search lamp?

Tell me, once the house unbinds
will my words grow back
weightier than a crucible
seep into your pocket
find in the light's dark pool
that one bright kiss that saves?

## You are sighing

your last farewell.
I am not ready, may never be.

How do we account for a life
built on a bulldozed plain
resurrect a boy
burdened by loss
the search for a mother
resurrect the half sums
make them come right?

You are ninety years old
have outlived two wives, an only son
never been sure you're lovable
pin your longing to the birds
your garden golden with forsythia
the faithful return of the strawberries.

The connoisseur of good jazz, crab cakes
Yankee ball wins, plain spoken politics
finally will you rise up triumphant
vouched safe
home?

You are saying goodbye

to your gusty prayer book
blueberry bushes
newspapers, jazz

no longer winding the hands
of your German clock
dishing up cat chow.

You are closing
the perch of your mouth that
has been an epicure's apprentice
field troubled with rodents.

You are wielding your body
toward a new door
that doesn't speak orphaned

minding your tongue
of its pitchforks
digging down
and down
and down

to gather that broken boy
mired in clay.

## You are calling back

your dead wives
the winning season of Yankees
your only son
calling back the fortune teller
with her crystal globe
bribable future

on your bed in the middle of the living room
you are calling out winning bids
for your last hand of pinochle
calling across an ocean to Australia
to your only daughter and granddaughter
*bring them home*

tell me on the phone
even in your last hours
*I will wait.*

You have always been

a damned up tear
hurt so big the sea winces
blind man amid stones
who walks on stilts
till the stilts splinter.

How does the oak survive
the maul of winter
the orchard come back to bear fruit
the bird with the torn wing
move from fence to tree
manage to lift
into the blue rise
still bright
hopeful as Christmas?

My father carries a cross

up on his shoulders like a cradle
carries it invisible
will not burden you with its tears
wounded sunlight
ask for proof the world is decent
the women he has loved, married
still care.

He knows things can drown
get buried
cancer sets up its own death camp
end rhymes don't always shine
on a silver plate.

My father carries a cross
from room to room
dime store to cafe
blurts out words
as if the wind still listens
the truth has no holes.

## I won't always need to coax

till your words melt
your boots no longer muck
my house with their gravel

won't always sing off key
keep my heirlooms hidden
till blades rescind
the day arrives clear of arrows.

Some seasons are heavy wool
an ice storm
some seasons are a tease parade
frivolous poppies
the beggarly hymnbook.

Look at me
look at me just this once
as a vein of good ore
decency
don't cast my shape into one of
your anonymous death notes.

In my sleep

I search splintered streets
a cathedral
to taste the salt
of my father's limbs

find him alone in a squat bed
his face weary
eyes wet.

When I ask what has happened
my father's mouth
is a net with no words
below the halo.

In the clear light of the early dawn

my father is making his way
to a new place
has not been there before
nibbled its corn
laid his body out
is not particularly willing
but a hand insists, guides
reminds *the future is a hymn of grass.*

I have known him to go slow
make an art out of careful penmanship
make special the grilled cheese sandwich
have known him to amp up Argentine jazz
when the night turns lonely.

Not many find time to notice him
as he hobbles along with his walker
not everyone is patient
admires the sheen of his head
freckled hands, sloped body
face valleyed with wrinkles
notices his pleasure in touching a peony
smelling the saffron

the way he lowers his lips to the fruit
of the blueberry bush and teases.

Are there days when
the world renders us invisible
nobody seems curious
about our time in the war
first kiss in Manhattan
home baked crumb cake
nobody notices the holes in our hands
the way a punctured landscape
can resemble a face
how decency never really wants to
walk abroad with a big stick?

My father is threading his way
toward an unknown future
at 90 years old looks out of place in this hip city
where nobody ever ages
is hauling his shopping bags, food coupons
across the busy roadway
grumbling to me about the election
global warming

recent floods in the South
our current heat wave
talking Coltrane, German bratwurst
his vote for Bernie

how good it feels
with all his aches and pains
the in and out of his catheters
the advanced prostate cancer
lump growing on his right lung
to still be here

his June strawberries heavy on the vine
the new Best of Judy Garland CD waiting
each cup of coffee, slice of cheesecake
pinochle hand
precious.

In the dry mouth of the day's cottonwoods

my father is practicing his new voice
its high and lows
desolate and sunset
practicing spring's romp past fern flanked trees
the hush of his mother's deathbed.

In the dry mouth of the day's cottonwoods
my father is reshaping his mouth
into a different story
where the boy gets swooped up by relations
avoids an orphanage
no one points a finger
slaps him hard on the face.

In the dry mouth of the day's cottonwoods
my father wants to reinvent his last act
before the careless wind sets in
before he arrives at my brother's limp body

is trying to reshape his mouth
mimic the jackdaw cawing in the tree
the purr of the neighbor's cat
the last of the summer raspberries
gone ripe.

I want you to last forever

not doze in a sleep that lengthens
grow so weak your catheters
can't find you
not dim beyond your mind's
highly evolved map work

want to watch you play pinochle
toast and butter your seeded bagel
warm the stew on the stove
keep the milestones turning
as if every tyrant can be put right
shine clear in an undimmed window

want the hours elastic
birds prolific in the tree
every flower you have ever loved
in bloom now
swollen with dew
wide eyed
faithful.

## My father collected coins and stamps

pressed them into waxy sleeves
to keep their surfaces clean
collected postcards from days
when Sundays were a park stroll
ladies wore curls, powder white gloves
prams were a lace trimmed
shelter for babies

collected Yankee ball cards
limited edition plates with nostalgic
scenes of children
German Hummel figures
dinner sets depicting Norman Rockwell
homegrown family mealtimes
he'd never known.

Tucked away in the corner of the basement
where my parents slept
my father would play Count Bassie
carefully unwrap his plates
admire each one, then put it back
use a magnifying glass to gaze at the stamps.

My brother and I tried to keep
out of his hair, impatience
too many jobs, wounded childhood

played outside till the dinner bell rang
and our mother's voice came reaching.

What did we know of the way
he secretly gathered beauty
preserved it stamp by stamp
plate by plate
imagined the summer he might have known
given a life away from that orphanage
the dead mother, drunken father
supper table of roast chicken, mashed potato
a family's laughter he might have shared
no sister snatched away forever
everybody glad for his presence
the table setting on the left earmarked
especially for him.

Were you always the knobby groom

minding a blue exit
single place setting

did she tease, deride you
deconstruct your imperialism
make for an ornate tea party
burdened with lavender
under the bed sheets?

## You cast your eye over the field

reduce it to *a damaged thing*
periled corn
child's angular wish list

sticker your precious onto
the machine's big tongue

but it is for you
my mother breaks open
her body
anoints your life
with more than tar pitch
a forlorn nest.

Were there times

under the shade tree
she'd call you to prayer
a scarlet sunset
jays in the tree
bid you to holy

did her body shimmy
out of that black sheath
draw you to a different
measure of moonlight
as if you were her one and only
one and only

her red lipstick
inked across your body
you a blank slate
about to come alive
in her classroom?

# Part Six

*The Welcoming Forest*

## My father is holding a candle

that burns phosphorous
who is to tell him
his daughter leaks blood
is a product of loss, malnutrition
who is to call his name
admit defeat at a deathbed?

Will the father let the girl
find a faith deeper than penance
unburden the dark of its stab wounds?

All night the moon sits viscous
lament wears a dark robe.
My father holds a candle.

Is it his last wish to see his daughter
unblotched by the ink pad
a moment where she can rise up
inimitable
beyond the pale?

## My father would gift give

then relent
pull back the dessert plate at table
cast me off as a burden
for sloshing the gravy.
There were times
no sweet scented act of mine
could appease him.

But it is good to know the world
runs on more than catastrophe
the weight of scales.
Spring comes.
It comes.
Be ready for the snowdrops
first stammer of crocus
lives with such a brief season
bound by faith.

What does the word *naught* stand for

is it more than a filling station
sucked dry of fuel
the armless pinwheel?

When my father lost his job at forty
he pinned *naught* onto his chest
dragged its weight
wrote over 150 job applications
nabbed only one interview.

What does the word *naught* say
when it can no longer crowd please
turn the drought into friend
does it scrape our plate
begging for sunset
memorize the place stars once blazed?

In the eye of God
does *naught* stand for the empty field
decommissioned mouth
place where the last ride first
the unequipped
find a home?

## Things come and go

remind me of my mother
her stabs of pain
as she paced back and forth
in that hospital
was misdiagnosed
two weeks later vanished

remind me of the way
the prom dress I wore senior year
with its empire waist, pert lavender
hint of a balconied future
was always meant for somebody else
how the day feels
when it's stripped down
world smacked
no longer sexy

remind me of paisley dance halls
gorilla warfare, bedlam, lust
the ill formed and half fabricated
my once lives that pass by in a flash
as I rock and rock and rock
remember the men who preoccupied me
became lovers and confidantes
became rain slicked and farewells
became the knife that cuts and the
precious of valentines

remember myself as something truer
sweeter, brave, clear
protected in a certain perch
beyond cellophane

how the years go by
go by
ensnarl, entreat, confound
the way my brother drops dead
in an anonymous hotel room
my children suckle, then grow
till they are young adults
have lives of their own
their own rocking chairs

how the stories we pile up
shift, dislodge
grow pantyhose with a sea of runs
grow gardens of lupine, honeysuckle
grow cucumbers, heirloom tomatoes
bolted spinach, a slug colony

how we rock and rock
till maybe some days we *are*
Gibraltar
the rock of Sisyphus

the hour of someone's revenge
the green risk of algae
coral cup of a wolf's hunger

we rock and rock
as if the centuries can hold
God rides a durable turntable
where no hour is better or worse
than this one
the forest, the raked meadow
bluesy couple
child in my rear view mirror
my father's sizzle of garlic with the potato
are enough.

When mercy comes

rummages through my room
turns my tears into an ice rink
let it not be fickle

a dialog of broken bones
the dime store bride
in search of a cake top

let there be slow time
no more shame disguised as a limp.

When mercy comes
wider than table manners
genuflection

let me offer you up my paw
shy girl in a print dress
steer you home
to the welcoming forest.

Your polestar is waiting

bright in a distant field
waits on your worn face
as the women wait
the river answers.

It has not always been this clear
the chronicle of doves
whippoorwills
amid the mourning.

Your polestar is waiting
will offer up silver streaks
corned beef on rye
a peace treaty against pain
endless hands of poker.

Beyond the orphanage, abuse
you return now to the child
you left behind

learn to ride a bike
lick the dark silly
slip onto your mother's lap
as if all is forgiveness.

A diamond cutter's apprentice

my father has had a hard time
learning his trade
put it down to big hands
strained eyesight
a heart desperate
for mothering.

Every anniversary with death
is a reason he dreams.

My father has always said *when my boat comes in, I want to be ready*

To this end we kept musty orange lifejackets and a pair of oars propped in the garage. They didn't cramp things since we never owned a boat or car and my father didn't know how to drive.

Hollis, Queens is not the most plush place to grow up. There are dumps for garbage, dumps for dog poop, and then general dumps to slide down in boxes. My mom had a wire cart on wheels to get the groceries. When I was six, swooning along in her tight dress and spike heels, she realized that nothing much was going to ever get better. Later she'd send postcards, first from Cape Cod, then Colorado Springs, then Truckee, California, then San Diego where rumor has it she found a guy who drowned in her Liz Taylor looks, happened to have a house near Tahoe and two decent cars. But that lasted only a few years.

My aunt Joan says it's not her fault she left us, that something got screwed up in her artsy fartsy head back when she was little. None of the other relations where willing to talk about it.
My dad always reminds me-*don't ever mention her name in my house*- my being the key word since my

brother and I have always felt like vagrant guests about to be tossed out.

But I guess none of this matters now since we are both grown up with some form of depression, know the world is not very pine scent clean, but ravaged with the loss of insects, warfare, acres of forests reduced to flame.

I'm going to the community college and it takes two jobs and three roommates to make it work. Am studying to be a dental hygienist with decent pay. My brother smokes, snorts stuff but I don't want to go there, talk about how he busts his butt in hard slog jobs for fifty hour weeks then smokes away his paycheck on the weekend. It causes pain in my heart since my mom passed away too soon, too many miles away for either of us to deal with.

When my father's boat comes in, and I know it's going to, I want to be alive, not drugged out, flashlight in hand willing to help him steer out of every fog that has ever blinded him.
My brother tells me I have a pie eyed version of God, a savior's complex, will eat up the woodwork to find one morsel of cheese worth saving. I don't know about that, know only that the nuns, with

their orthopedic shoes and strict words, never saved me. If there were gold crypts behind the altar they were always meant for somebody else.

But I do know one day there will be a boat. Nothing particularly fancy. My father will pick up his dust coated oars and row, not inflicted with wounds, but row steady as if his life depends on it. He will embrace the summer rain, listen to my words as if they hold seed instead of thistle. And on this day I will grant him the key to my innermost room as if he's never done anything bad, never shamed me or stolen my one good dress.

On this day, July will burn bright in the middle of a heat wave. My mother will be waiting, not on a precipice but somewhere on the beach, her hair wild with wind and sand. And with courage I will help guide that boat my father has been dreaming of, help him catch sight of her body's beacon, navigate the waves, help him see her as not something aberrant, diseased
but salt stained, the sound in his soul missing, the first and the last come home.

More than the wounded soldier

who carries a widower's cross
the rub of abscess
my father will come to you
bearing pot roast, pudding
ball scores

come to you
as if his torn limbs
have grown back
the sky knows how to
move past thunder
stay soft.

In real life

my daughter and I rushed
through Australian air terminals
frantic to get back
to my father's dying bed.
Too many delays.
We never made it.

In my dream he says
with a periled voice
*it is time to go*
and then vanishes
leaving me daisies
a clutch of boxes.

Tear stained
I open one of them.
Inside a pair of wooden shoes
that cup my feet like a nest.
Are they to travel me the many miles
over the ocean of life?
What would it be like to be free?

No more blurred kiss

then a spotty sweater
mud boots to put right
the blighted field
fashion you defenseless.

Now every woman
holds a flame
etched flute
untarnished mind
from the other kingdom.

July keeps no tally
damage control
crushed daisies
does not halter the girl
in the blue dress
turn her into a
death wish.

## Farewell

No apologies.
I have been a gravedigger
guardian of holes
timekeeper for the deceased
fallen shelf of possibility.

Farewell
camera ready art
slick magazines
windows with their blinds shut

farewell girl in the curio shop
among the sucked lemons
skeletal tightrope.

Farewell.

## Farewell my Soldier

So many tissue layers of kisses
gone rancid
so many tar pitch words
unsaid ones.

Farewell my bull dog
chain gang
early morning finch
corridor of hacked weeds
blue palsy.

Farewell wanting to show you
my fluted geography
reams of poems
choir practice.

How many years
to shore up a life
let it sing in its own Abigail?

Farewell my father
of the invisible wounds
shellshock.
By now you should know
I loved you.
Rest in peace.
Rest in peace.

I can move on now

unstop my throat
move on to days
no longer polished
beyond the peril.

See how I refuse to
crowd please
screw my voice into a socket

how the put right dawn feels
when every ray of sun
confirms me
listens.

## Listen

It was not always sane.
Some only saw the charmed voice.
Some nights were a disguise
of stab wounds.

But in the makeshift
of this world
even the gnat is entitled
to her stabs of glory
the moon to a silvered mouthpiece

the girl with the brown chimera
to her season of seashells
life beyond the Bismarck.

Can innocence set up

its own pearled kingdom
make for restful nights
a housecoat named poppy

can it mend my childhood
marriage
arrive with dumplings, tea
the promise of faithful

can innocence
wipe the dark clean
serenade us with sheep?

Can days always be this calm

speechless
no longer a walk the dog
of my heart elsewhere
territory of collisions

can they multiply
a testament to endurance
to sheets, delicate lingerie
flapping *yes* in the noonday sun

can they become lullaby
mercy steaming from every manhole
the white orchestration of snowflakes

each and every one of them
no longer a blue sermon
but precious
here and now and forever
beautiful?

Back then

I would trouble the day
for its hasty
travel cake batter
pots of jam
a tallow boat

back then
the day fought to contain me
its hurt clauses
blue sentences

but still the stars heaved
the night sky counseled
still river women
gifted me with mussels
speckled the stars
onto my dress.

Are there shorelines

with no soiled wings
contamination
where children collect shells
scoop water
know love as more than
a forked tongue
crushed daisy?

You have taken me
to a new country.
The air smells clean
moonlight no longer dangles.

Even I, who have stayed up
the centuries trying to calm you
can rest now
unabridged.

My father is combing the dark

with his fingers
picking lint off
my spotty jacket
placing a host on my tongue
that is beyond denial
beyond name-calling.

He is combing the dark
careful with his fingers
chronicling his love
in the key of fruit trees
deer, spider, sheep
a kingdom where the last
come first
every child knows a home.

My father is combing the dark
in the name of what's been forgotten
aborted, survives
even in a hailstorm.

He is combing my words
into fleece.

# Glory

My father is crowning my head
with his glory.
It wasn't always like this
his hands leading me through
the sedge, bramble
hasn't always been the moon
with a gilded mouthpiece.

My father has been removing
the locust that plague things
is crowning my head with his glory.
This has taken a long time.

Who would I be to turn away
such gift
in the name of loss?

Toni Thomas lives in Portland, Oregon. Her poems have been published in Austria, Spain, New Zealand, Canada, England, Scotland, and Australia. In the United States her work has appeared in over fifty literary magazines including *Prairie Schooner, North Dakota Quarterly, Hayden's Ferry Review, the Minnesota Review, Notre Dame Review, Poetry East,* and more. She has been twice nominated for a Pushcart prize, and won several awards. She has published twenty-five collections of poetry and six books for children.

Her figurative clay sculptures have been shown in gallery exhibits in Portland and Chicago, displayed in literary magazines, and housed in private collections in the U.S. and England.

Her short documentary *One of Us* was shown at the Trans-ideology: Nostalgia festival in Berlin and at the Museum of Contemporary Art in Taipei.

Since Toni loves to create and sits buried in reams of poems, manuscripts, clay figures and images....she likes to imagine all of them out in the world swaying wild as the lupine.

tonithomaspoetry.com

www.ingramcontent.com/pod-product-compliance
Lightning Source LLC
Chambersburg PA
CBHW030440010526
44118CB00011B/728